LONDON GOES TO WAR - 1939

LONDON GOES TO WAR - 1939

by Gordon Bromley

London
MICHAEL JOSEPH

First published in Great Britain by
Michael Joseph Ltd, 52 Bedford
Square, London WC1
1974

ISBN 0 7181 1140 0

Printed in Great Britain by Butler
& Tanner Ltd, Frome, Somerset,
on paper supplied by Gerald Judd
Ltd and bound by Dorstel Press,
Harlow

Contents

Preface

London Goes To War gives a vivid picture of life in London at the outbreak of war and the months that followed. In words and pictures it shows how ordinary people adapted their lives to wartime conditions and how the face of London changed. It is the first book of its kind to do so.

In the first few days of September, 1939, nearly six hundred thousand London children were evacuated. Trenches were dug in the parks. Buildings were heavily sandbagged. Anderson shelters went up in hundreds of thousands of gardens. Gas masks were the order of the day. Auxiliary firemen learnt to run out hose and carry one another down ladders. In every street air raid wardens instructed their neighbours what to do when the siren sounded. Doctors, nurses, ambulance men, all stood by for the countless casualties expected at any moment. And every night London was engulfed in a complete blackout, making it sometimes seem like a city of the dead.

Then after a few weeks when the raids did not materialise, there was a sense of anti-climax. Life in many ways returned to normal. Many of the children came home. Businesses which had closed opened up again. So did places of entertainment. Football returned—with the pools! Blackout restrictions were not observed quite so strictly. By Christmas, more theatres were open than there had been a year before.

The somewhat easier conditions of life continued till the spring, when Hitler attacked in the West. Soon Londoners began to see Norwegian, Dutch, Belgian, French refugees, followed by their own troops back from Dunkirk. And, after that, planes going over to fight the Battle of Britain. They guessed then their turn would follow next. And it did. On Saturday, September 7th, 1940, came the first full-scale raid. The opening phase of London's war was over. Now London was in the front line. What happened then makes an exciting story, too. But it cannot eclipse the memory of the months before—the twelve months covered by this book.

The pictures in this book taken by the cameramen of the weekly magazine "Illustrated" have not previously been published.

Acknowledgments

For this book I have relied largely on government publications, newspapers of the time and personal recollections—my own and those of friends and acquaintances. I have also found much useful information in the following books, to the authors of which I am grateful: *The People's War* by Angus Calder, *The Phoney War on the Home Front* by E S Turner, *Backs to the Wall* by Loenard Mosley, *The Blitz* by Constantine Fitzgibbon, *Collected Essays, Journalism and Letters* by George Orwell, *The Second World War* by Winston Churchill, *The Day War Broke Out* by Ronald Deth, *London Front* by F Tennyson Jesse, *Prime Time—the Life of Ed Murrow* by Alexander Kendrick, *Problem of Social Policy* by R M Titmuss *The Home Guard* by Charles Graves, *Soldiering On* by General Sir Hubert Gough. I am especially indebted to *War Begins at Home*, a Mass Observation book edited by Tom Harrisson and Charles Madge.

'It *must* be war this time.' The first of September, when Hitler invaded Poland, was a Friday. Londoners on their way home flocked to Westminster to watch Parliament assemble. This was a turning point in history and they wanted to see those who were making the big decisions. They were quiet but inwardly, of course, excited. What would they be doing this time next week? Would they even be alive? It looked, at any rate, as though there would be a break from the office routine of nine to six. All through the weekend, crowds pressed round the railings. Others were glued to their radio sets at home, waiting for the news that war had been declared.

Facing Hitler
at last

L ondon would be destroyed. In the first twenty-four hours thousands of bombs would pound it to rubble. Millions of people would be killed—blown to pieces, burnt or poisoned by gas. There was no escape. Had not Baldwin stated categorically 'The bomber will always get through', Chamberlain that if another war came we must all expect to be in the line of fire? And Attlee—and scores of others—that another war would be the end of civilisation? Look what had happened in Spain—at Guernica. Look what was happening now—in Poland. Hitler was a maniac, power-mad. He had the mightiest air force in the world, ready to bomb anyone or anything. If we declared war, it was all too clear what he would do. He would act fast, before the effect of our blockade could be felt, aiming for a knock-out. And there was only one place for that: London.

These were the thoughts in people's minds in September 1939, during the two days between the invasion of Poland and the British declaration of war.

The threat had, of course, been there the year before. But then it had not come to anything. Mr Chamberlain, with

The luckier ones were there when the King and Prime Minister came out of Number Ten together. During the coming uneventful months King George and Queen Elizabeth, by their visits to units in all parts of London, did a good job in keeping up the spirits of civil defence workers. Mr Chamberlain, though still supported by the bulk of the conservative party, was too closely associated with Munich to be universally popular. Once Germany and Russia had overrun Poland many thought he might still try to patch up yet another peace with Hitler.

All eyes were on Churchill. For ten years he had been out of office and consistently the most vehement critic of the government's foreign policy. Now all his warnings about the threat from Nazi Germany had come true. Unknown to the watching crowds, Chamberlain, within hours of the attack on Poland, had already offered him a place in the new war cabinet and two days later was to ask him to take charge of the Admiralty. Many people, as they saw him on that Friday afternoon, wished Churchill rather than Chamberlain was prime minister.

umbrella, had returned from Munich, waving his piece of paper. 'I believe it is peace for our time' he had said. The evacuated children had been brought back from the country. The sandbags taken down in Whitehall. The trenches, dug in the parks, boarded over. The bombs never fell. But things like that do not happen twice. This time it would be different. This time there would be no more negotiations. No more aeroplane trips for Mr Chamberlain. This time war must surely be here.

All the same, for most Londoners, mixed with dread was a feeling of relief, relief that at last we were about to make a stand. Ever since 1933, when the Nazis took power, it had been one act of aggression, one international crisis after another. Each time, after Hitler had got what he wanted, he made further demands. Clearly, it could not go on for ever. Sooner or later the demands would come so close we should have to fight or become part of the Nazi world. So would not it be better to go to war now than hang on yet another year or two with this ominous shadow destroying our courage and self-respect? Many after Munich had felt a sense of guilt. Morally,

Below: Another place that drew the crowds—as always at times of national emergency—was Buckingham Palace. Not just to see the changing of the guard, of course. Soldiers had their jackets off and were putting up sandbags and conical-shaped steel shelters for the sentries, ready for when the bombs began to fall. Quite a lot of those who watched, having studied the technique, went home and did some sandbagging of their own. Luckily, it was fine, sunny weather—ideal for this sort of operation. Indeed, the fine weather lasted all through September.

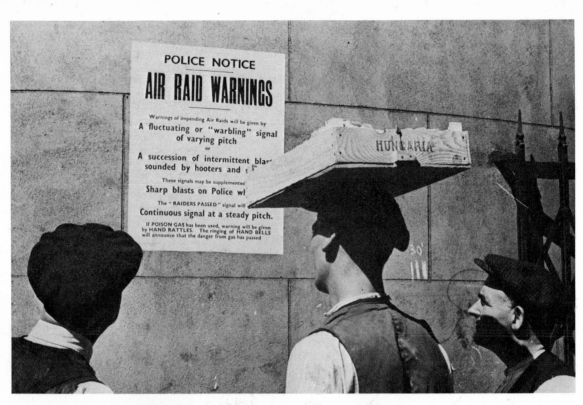

had not we and the French been under an obligation to help defend Czechoslovakia? Instead, we had made an agreement nearly everyone—if not Mr Chamberlain—knew Hitler would not keep. It was too late to save the Czechs but less than six months ago we had told the Nazis that if they invaded Poland they would be at war with us. They had invaded Poland. So this was it.

Dread, however much tempered by relief, hardly leads to high spirits, and Londoners that weekend were quiet and subdued. There was no outward excitement as there had been in 1914. No shouting or singing. No waving of union jacks. Just waiting, that was all.

At a quarter past eleven on Sunday morning, 3 September, 1939, Chamberlain made his famous broadcast, stating war had been declared. He had hardly finished when the air-raid sirens ('sireens' as so many Londoners always called them) started to wail. As people trooped off to the shelters they had been digging furiously in the last few days some complained the Nazis must have cheated and got their planes into the air before the declaration. 'Typical' they said, then listened for the first ack-ack, the first bombs. It was all tremendously quiet—rather like the pre-war two minutes silence when armis-

Top left: Some time or other war might come, of course—Londoners had long realised that—but seeing the air raid warning notices in their own streets really brought home to them that 'sometime or other' was now. At any moment they must expect to hear 'warbling' sounds on the sirens or short blasts on police whistles, telling them to take shelter. The air raid notices in the streets were, of course, repeated ad infinitum in the newspapers and on the radio. It didn't take people long to learn the message of the sirens.

Bottom left: Over the weekend, since raids were expected any moment, bobbies on duty were ordered to wear tin hats. Their white sleeves, too, came in useful during the blackout—when motorists, driving with only a glimmer of light, all too often showed a recklessness that was quite inexcusable, sometimes showing a 'priority' label on their windscreens to which they were not entitled. With the duties of air-raid wardens and other civil defence workers sometimes overlapping those of the police, there were occasional misunderstandings, but generally speaking these were ironed out easily enough.

Right: Coming as it did, in the first week of September, the outbreak of war coincided with many Londoners' holidays. Some felt themselves lucky to have booked accommodation well away from what might be a doomed city. Others, as this picture shows, found their arrangements had been cancelled. Yet others did the cancelling themselves, preferring to join the civil defence, dig shelters and be on the spot, ready to protect their homes from incendiary bombs. Older people with gardens, remembering food shortages in the First World War, started digging up lawns and flower beds in preparation for vegetables.

Below: Sentries suddenly appeared on bridges, at entrances to tunnels and outside key buildings. Did the government expect German paratroops? Or were the sentries on guard against a 'Fifth Column'? This expression, ascribed to a general in the Spanish Civil War only a year or two earlier, was very widely used at the time. In London, during the last few months not much had been seen or heard of Fascist or Nazi sympathisers, but who knew what damage they might try to do now war had broken out?

tice day was strictly observed. But, mysteriously as it seemed at the time, the guns never fired, the bombs never fell. Quite soon the all clear sounded and everyone came out into the sunshine again. The general feeling was it must have been a rehearsal by our civil defence people to let us all get used to taking cover (the real explanation that an unidentified French plane had caused the alarm was not generally known till later).

Surprised, many of them, to be still alive, people grinned at each other and mostly carried on with what they had been doing before the warning sounded. Some cooked the Sunday dinner. Some went off to the pub. Some who had gone to church, where in many cases radio sets had been installed for the broadcast, said a prayer. Some went to see their families. Some drove off for what, they felt, might be a last look at the English countryside.

The fine, sunny day ended and London slept. And then, at three o'clock in the morning, the sirens sounded again. 'Ah, this is the real thing' people said, trailing out to the shelters or crouching under the stairs or wherever they felt was the safest place. 'They're starting while it's dark and then at dawn they'll have the sun behind them so our boys won't be able to see them properly.' But once again nothing happened.

So ended what was for many Londoners the most surprising twenty-four hours of the war.

Left: At the start, what many—perhaps most—Londoners dreaded above all was gas. In the Munich crisis they had all been issued with gas-masks and the thought that some time they might have to wear them had been with them ever since. Now they were told to get used to wearing them for half-an-hour or so each day. They were hot and smelly and most people found the experience so distasteful and unpleasant that it's doubtful if they kept them on for more than a few minutes.

Left: People carried their gas-masks about in various ways. Some, like the gentleman with the ladder, simply wrapped them up in their cardboard boxes and attached them to their normal impedimenta. Others, like the GPO boy, had smart cylindrical cases. A wide range of containers—some of them expensive—appeared in West End shops, designed to go with fashionable coats and dresses. They became quite a topic of conversation but by spring 1940 very few people were carrying them.

Below: For children under the age of two a special type of container was issued. This went right over the head and the upper part of the body, filtered air being supplied by bellows. Few mothers dared to imagine what would happen if the gas ever came. A small minority made gas-proof rooms in their homes, sealing up windows, ventilators and chimneys. When there were no raids, let alone gas, the whole thing became a rather sour joke and an enormous number of masks were lost or mislaid.

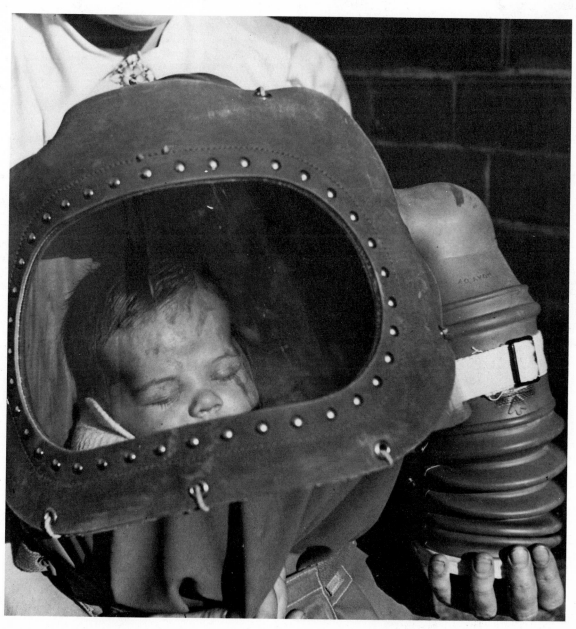

Below: Sometimes there seemed even more uniformed women—Wrens, Ats, Waafs, Women of the Mechanised Transport Corps and the rest. It was certainly very different from 1914, when the idea that women—apart from nurses—should wear uniform was quite revolutionary. Now, it was taken for granted.

Right: The West End seemed full of soldiers, sailors and airmen—on duty in London itself or on their way to join their units—but all, of course, with service respirators slung across their shoulders. These looked much more substantial than the civilian type and made many citizens wonder if their own masks were really much good.

In many ways it was a good time to be a boy scout. At least there was a chance for adventure and you felt you were doing something that really mattered, with adults depending on you. Scouts acted as messengers for the fire service, rescue squads and first aid parties and made themselves generally useful in innumerable ways. Some of them proved they knew more about knots than the firemen, more about first aid than the ambulance people.

Top: Anti-aircraft guns, sticking up menacingly from Hyde Park, Hampstead Heath and other normally peaceful places, soon became an accepted part of wartime London. Since there were no enemy planes to fire at, nothing was heard from them till nearly a year later. It was different with the searchlight batteries. Wandering about in the black-out, Londoners might suddenly see the whole sky lit up with wheeling columns of radiance, as the searchlight men went into action, testing their organisation and apparatus. For a few minutes perhaps the marvellous show would be on. Then, suddenly as it started it would be over, as though a single switch had turned out all the lights.

Bottom: At some A.A. sites there was ingenious camouflage. This art had developed enormously during World War I but in 1939, since London did not expect a land attack, all camouflage related to what could be seen from the air. Vast quantities of paint and other materials were used to transform the roofs of factories and other key buildings in the hope that the raiders would not only fail to spot their targets but completely lose their way. Unfortunately, there was one thing that could not be camouflaged: the River. So long as the Germans could see that, they would always have a rough idea of where they were.

Tents among the deckchairs seemed reminiscent of fairgrounds and bank holidays rather than anything to do with war. All sorts of people were under canvas in London's parks and open spaces that September: trench diggers, A.A. gunners, searchlight operators, balloon barrage men among them. It wasn't a bad place to be—the skies were blue, the trees beginning to get their autumn colour and there were always plenty of friendly people ready to bring out a thermos flask or sandwiches or perhaps just pass the time of day.

The balloons go up

The most extraordinary sight in London at the start of war was the barrage of hydrogen-filled balloons, whose function was to discourage dive-bombers and low-level attacks. Forty or so of these balloons had been seen in London's sky during an exercise the year before but now the number had been increased and when people came out of their shelters after the all clear that first Sunday morning, the sky seemed full of them. Apart from doing the job for which they were intended, they proved of great psychological benefit to the citizens in the streets below. Many developed a superstitious faith in them, believing they had almost magical powers. Their potency was one of the reasons given by women returning to London from evacuation zones. Mass Observation reported such comments as:

'They look after us so well here, the balloons and that, they'll never get through.'

'I wouldn't be out of London for a hundred pounds. We're so well protected here.'

'I felt so unprotected there' (in the country), 'like anything might happen.'

Perhaps part of the appeal of the balloons, for some people at any rate, was that they were so purely defensive. Fighter planes and anti-aircraft guns were destructive. The balloons were gentle, amiable things that gave full warning of their presence and merely said 'please leave us alone'.

Left: The balloons going up was a fascinating spectacle. One moment the sky was empty. A few minutes later filled with these fantastic objects, reflecting the sunlight on their silver sides. They had quite a charming appearance—not suggesting war at all but rather as though they were part of some great fair or exhibition. They were particularly attractive at dawn or sunset when the low, rosy light shone on their undersides. In high winds they sometimes gave the crews a lot of trouble and occasionally got loose. And at odd times in thunderstorms they were struck by lightning.

Immediately below: The balloons, when grounded, looked rather different—more like strange creatures from a science fiction novel. They were generally anchored to trucks and serviced and wound up and down by crews of the RAF's special balloon command. (Later, as the demand for man-power in the armed forces grew, some of the work—though arduous enough—was taken off their hands by women) All sorts of stories got about as to how the balloons functioned. Mass Observation reported one man as saying that the barrage was electrified and drew aeroplanes like magnets, bombs being attracted by the cables and sliding harmlessly down them.

Bottom: This particular balloon's home was the Embankment Gardens but they were stationed in all kinds of open spaces. A favourite name for them was 'blimps' after the blown-out Colonel Blimp created by David Low, whose anti-Hitler cartoons in 'The Evening Standard' gave Londoners so much satisfaction before—as well as during—the war. 'Blimps' was a generic term. People also gave their own local balloons individual names such as 'Bimbo' or 'Bubbles'. They made friends, too, with the balloon crews and entertained them in their homes when they were off duty.

Taking cover

As with gasmasks, so with air-raid shelters—Londoners had had twelve months to get used to the idea. At the time of Munich, trenches—which had never been filled in—had been dug in the parks and many basements in public buildings had been strengthened. More shelters of various kinds were ready now and in the last few days before the war the work was frantically accelerated.

To prevent people crowding together, which might lead to many being killed by a single bomb, as well as to the spread of epidemics and, of course, to save treasury expenditure, government policy was to encourage individuals to provide their

own protection. By early September, nearly a million and a half Anderson shelters had been distributed, free of charge to those with incomes under £250 a year and most of these had been erected, either by the owners themselves or by the local councils. Where the gardens were small they took up most of the space. They were normally sunk three feet into the ground and enterprising gardeners built up the earth round to make them look less hideous. At the outbreak of war many supported fine shows of asters and tobacco plants. At that time people were glad to have them but, when the weather broke, they became less enthusiastic. 'Better take a chance of being bombed than run the certainty of pneumonia' was a common attitude. Certainly the thought of turning out from a warm bed in the middle of the night and stepping down into a cold, wet shelter was not inviting. Fortunately, that first winter the shelters were not needed—at least not for protection against bombs. They came in very handy, though, for storing garden tools and coal, keeping beer and housing rabbits among other things. They were also sometimes favoured by courting couples and, when the rains came and they were flooded, provided training for auxiliary firemen in the use of their suction hose.

Besides distributing Andersons, the Home Office issued a pamphlet on how to make a garden trench for six people. This, they reckoned, one man should be able to dig single-handed in

Left: Filling sandbags could be arduous enough. Digging trenches was an even tougher job. These particular sappers were medical students but the job was being done by men in every walk of life. That was one of the pleasanter things about London then—the breakdown of class barriers, the feeling that 'we're all in it together,' doing the same job, ready to face the same dangers. In the winter of 1939–40 much of the camaraderie was lost but it returned with even greater intensity under the threat of invasion—and, above all, during the Blitz.

Below: In the first twelve months of the war large numbers of surface shelters were put up in the streets, not only in inner London but also in the suburbs. They were more substantial than they looked and though not proof against a direct hit could be very effective against blast. They certainly proved useful as temporary shelters later, during the Blitz, and saved many lives. Before then, they were used largely for ARP exercises, when wardens not only got to know their neighbours but learnt some of the principles of handling crowds and allocating breathing space.

Below: Many shopkeepers sandbagged their premises and strengthened their basements to give air-raid protection to their customers. This was not only generous and humane but good business, too. If raids were likely, people would rather go to a shop that offered protection than one that did not. Some big stores had their own air raid wardens and elaborate systems of control to shepherd customers into the basement. A good many shops were closed, with the windows completely boarded up. Messages were sometimes scrawled on, such as 'Called up O.H.M.S. Back as soon as we beat Hitler'.

Right: Thousands of families spent the first weekend filling sandbags. Everyone joined in—men, women and children. Apart from anything else, filling sandbags or digging trenches was better for the nerves than sitting still and wondering just how long before the bombs fell—and for the children, at any rate, it was all good fun. Many of them had never been to the sea and had the chance to dig in sand before. Where sand was not available, earth or rubble was used. Some enthusiasts got darkened hurricane lamps or other forms of shaded light and carried on long after blackout.

seven periods of three to four hours each. The trench was lined to prevent the walls falling in and there was a covered entrance with gas-proof curtains. It was estimated that the average cost was about £8.

You could not put up an Anderson or dig a trench if you had no garden, so many people tried to make at least one room in their home safe by sandbagging walls and boarding up windows. Others favoured the cupboard under the stairs. There might not be room for all the family to stretch their legs but, at least, they might be able to protect their heads—and perhaps pull their legs in for a moment when they heard the bombs swishing down. Basement flats, especially when they could be reinforced, became more desirable than penthouses with splendid views. Basements and cellars anywhere were, of course, remembered at a time when the Rotterdam raid was still news. Crypts of churches might be useful and, obviously, vaults of banks. Would bank managers, however, be prepared to take a risk with their clients' valuables?

There was also a lot of talk about sheltering in the Tubes. Official policy was to oppose this but later, when the Blitz came, it was found impossible to prevent it. Those who had been in Spain during the civil war insisted that the only shelters really worth having were deep underground and there was criticism of the government for not providing them.

Left: Sandbagging as a rule did not reach as high as this—normally not more than waist height. But this was a priority building—Westminster Hospital. Doctors and skilled nursing staff worked with everyone else, filling and putting up the bags. Mountains of sand were brought in from all round London, some from quite near. Substantial excavations, for example, were made on Hampstead Heath, just below Jack Straw's Castle. Not all sandbagging was up to army standards and within a few months a good deal of it collapsed under the stress of bad weather, but for the time being at any rate it gave people a sense of protection.

Below: At the time of Munich, trenches had been dug in Hyde Park, Kensington Gardens and other London parks. Entrances to these had been closed for a year but they were now reopened and further trenches dug. Much of the work was done by mechanical excavators—always an attraction for sightseers—but brawn and muscle were also required. Trenches were also dug in many famous sports grounds in the suburbs. Men who only the week before had been flourishing cricket bats or kicking footballs dug up the very turf on which they had been playing.

Below: Not many Anderson shelters were as cosy as this one, but it shows what could be done with ingenuity and skill. Veterans who remembered dugouts in Flanders took pride in showing a younger generation some of the tricks. The flooring was important. Apart from good boards, a bit of old lino or carpet could make it seem much more homely. And then there was lighting—an electric flex from the house was best but oil lamps came in handy and, of course, an oil stove on which to boil the kettle. 'Don't forget the first-aid kit' was a routine instruction and you were also reminded to keep an axe or spade handy in case you needed to dig your way out. Magazines and a pack of cards were also a good idea.

Right: Some of the best protection was given in factories. The basement shelter here, for example, at the Carrier Engineering Company's works, was of a highly sophisticated nature. It had gas-proof doors, steel-lined ceilings, electricity and water supplies and three separate telephone lines—also a decontamination section with self-contained hot and cold water showers, poison gas filters and ventilating plant. It was well stocked with food and there was a radio and a gramophone. Air raid drill at such a place was not too irksome and certainly gave a sense of security to those concerned.

It was realised that if raids became heavy, Government might have to do much of its work underground. This picture shows the entrance to an air-raid refuge at the Foreign Office. All over London vaults which had hitherto been used simply to file records were cleared and turned into shelters. Restaurants and hotels, too, advertised prominently the sure protection of their basements. At first this may have attracted custom but it was probably not a powerful inducement until the blitz.

Top right: For people who could not get to a basement or had no garden where they could put up an Anderson, the only thing to do was make their homes as safe as possible. Number one priority was to stick brown paper across windows to prevent glass splintering and, if there was a raid, pull the curtains. The danger from flying glass when bombs are falling is a very real one, as Londoners were to realise in 1940. Passengers caught in a train were advised to pull down the blinds and, if possible, lie on the floor.

Bottom right: Some people either could not—or made up their minds they would not—get up and go to shelters once they had turned in for the night. The wisest of these, while raids seemed likely, did as this girl and kept everything handy by the bed: siren suit or trousers and dressing gown, gum boots, gasmask, torch, sticking plaster, cotton wool, iodine and other medical supplies. You were advised that before going to bed you should turn off all gas taps and fill the bath with water; and, in the event of a raid, get under the stairs or lie close to a wall well away from the window and the risk of flying glass.

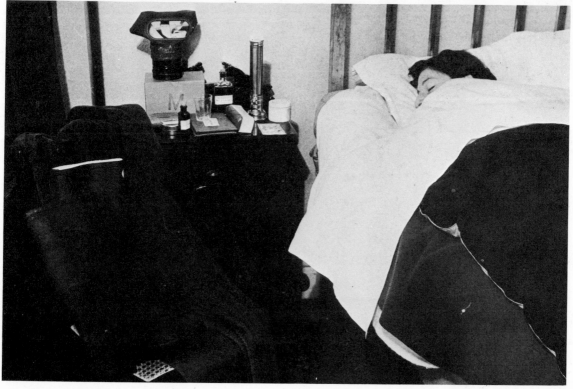

The children leave

Between 5.30 in the morning, Friday 1 September and midnight, Sunday 3 September, something like six hundred thousand children, accompanied by their teachers, left London for safe billets in the country. In the light of what was expected from air-raids, this was the only sensible and humane thing to do. Indeed, despite complaints about how evacuation worked, if the government had not made such arrangements there would have been a public outcry.

The movement of the children was on the whole carried out successfully enough. Buses to pick them up at the schools and take them to the stations were there to schedule. Queuing for the trains was orderly. Railwaymen of all grades worked overtime to make things run as smoothly as possible. It was a weekend when everybody wanted to do their best. The journey, too, allowing for all the circumstances, was generally pretty good. Some trains did not have corridors and lavatories. Sometimes the children had not brought enough food and supplies could not be augmented. Some who had to change trains at junctions got separated from their friends and ended up at destinations miles away from anyone they knew. But by and large it was not until the journey was over that the troubles began.

Early in 1939 the local authorities in the 'reception areas' had made a return of all homes where there was room for evacuees. Just how accurate these returns were it is impossible to know. Many people naturally wanted to reserve some at least of their rooms for children and aged members of their own families. Others simply wanted to avoid having evacuees of any sort. But, at any rate, wherever the trains arrived in September there were supposed to be enough beds in the neighbourhood for the number of children unloaded. Almost without exception this proved to be the case—partly because, when it came to the point, fewer children turned up for evacuation than was expected. But, of course, it was not only beds and food and shelter they needed, but love, friendship, homes to meet their mental and emotional needs. Where these were lacking, misery and bitterness, not surprisingly, followed.

The evacuation led to a tremendous mix-up of social classes which was often painful on both sides. Many of the children came from London's worst slums. They were, some of them, dirty, diseased, lice-infected. Everyone was sorry for them but most people did not want them to come and live with their own families. Conversely, there were children from comfortable homes who now found themselves in dark, damp cottages with primitive sanitation and no electric light. There were house-proud people who, understandably, no doubt, became angry when ill-brought-up children scratched beautiful furniture, muddied precious carpets and smashed delicate china. There were some who expected the children to behave as ser-

Goodbye London. How long before we see you again? The previous week there had been a dress rehearsal so nearly all knew what they were supposed to do and, generally speaking, everything went smoothly. However worried some of the children may have been, and however sad at leaving Mum and Dad, there was no doubt it was very exciting, a great adventure. Many surprises lay ahead, not all of them pleasant, but as they went on their way most children were in pretty good spirits. It was the parents, left at home, who at that particular time suffered most.

Right: On evacuation day the children met at their schools. Where were they going? Who were they going to stay with? Would they be billeted together with their friends? Or split up? How long before they saw their parents again? Would they ever see them again? Or would they be killed in air-raids? Dozens of questions like these must have gone through their minds as they set off that morning. They, no doubt, felt better when they got to school, away from their parents and among the gang. The boy in front in this picture seems hopeful of getting to the seaside. Otherwise, what's the bucket for?

Far right: All the girls and boys were supposed to bring hand luggage they could manage themselves, including gas-masks, a change of underwear, night clothes, shoes, spare stockings or socks, a toothbrush, a comb, a towel, soap, face cloth, handkerchief and, if possible a warm coat or macintosh. Also a packet of food to last the day. Each child and each piece of luggage had to have a name label. Destination, however, was unknown except to the authorities. All the children and parents were told was they were going 'somewhere safe'. It was very definitely a trip into the unknown.

Below: 'Makes a change from arithmetic, any way'. It was a hard day for teachers—with a heavy weight of responsibility. It was not just a matter of checking labels and luggage. There were all the problems of the journey, too. Most important of all, at the other end the teachers would be the only adults the children knew. They would have to answer all kinds of tricky questions and to a large extent take the parents' place in helping the children settle down in their new environment. Many teachers, some of them quite young, did a marvellous job at this crucial time.

Top right: Some billets were good. Some were not. Not all children got a foster-mother who tucked them up at night or had nice, clean sheets and running water in the bedroom. Many lacked affection at a time they needed it most and beds, mattresses and even blankets sometimes ran short. The whole thing was really a tremendous gamble. You might get conditions very much better than you were used to. They might be very much worse. Children from the same school who knew each other well got billeted in entirely different kinds of homes. Inevitably, this led to a good deal of jealousy.

Bottom right: Still with identity labels round their necks, these three set off to explore their new world—'somewhere in Essex'. For many London children it was their first experience of country life and the start of all kinds of new interests. They learnt about farms and animals, helped with the harvest, went blackberrying (mushrooming, too, if they were lucky) and in some cases developed a real interest in natural history. Their schoolroom education may have suffered but they certainly benefited in other ways, quite apart from the fresh air and sunshine.

vants and have their meals apart, in the kitchen. Still others maintained that the eight-and-sixpence a week they were paid by the authorities was not enough and vented their rage on the child. There were, on the other hand, many kind people who did all they could to make the children happy and started friendships with them that have lasted till today.

As well as the children, tens of thousands of adults left London. Many civil servants were dispatched to the provinces, often against their will. Quite a lot of businesses moved off. Old people with friends and relations in the country accepted invitations for the duration. And the rich paid fancy prices for homes in safe areas. Some went as far as the Dominions or the United States.

Apart from all this, London's population was considerably smaller than usual, owing to the lack of tourists. Because of the uncertain international situation during July and August, fewer had arrived from abroad than usual and nearly all who had come and had not yet got away were desperately trying to do so by the time war broke out.

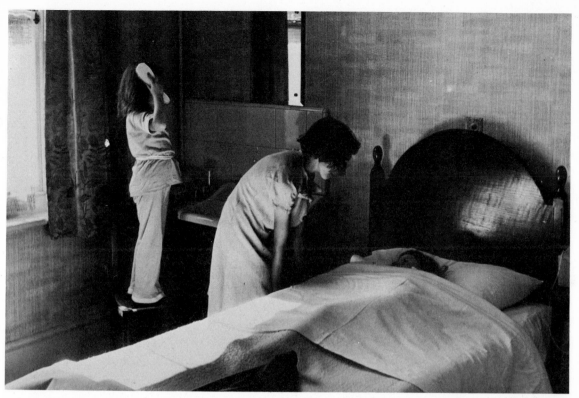

Top left: This little gang had been properly trained. Even paddling in the sea, miles from London, they still carried their gasmasks. After the first few weeks they probably were not so careful. Possibly not so happy, either. Many enjoyed the change at first but, especially as the summer turned to Autumn and they couldn't be out so much, soon wanted to get back home. After all, there had been no raids on London, so what was the point of staying away longer—especially when, obviously in most cases, their hosts and hostesses would be only too pleased to see the back of them. The kids missed cinemas, shops, fish and chips.

Bottom left: Arrangements were made so that children below school age could be accompanied by their mothers. That was fine, but what about the fathers left at home? Many remained devoted husbands and parents, of course. But others not only objected to doing their own cooking and housework but, without a wife to come home to in the evening, sought consolation with other women. There can be no doubt that evacuation led to the permanent break-up of many families and altered the course of many lives. Its effect on our society is still being felt.

Right: During the evacuation a tremendous job was done by the WVS—not only in taking care of the children during the journey but in helping to sort things out the other end. Women who had run their own homes and brought up their own families were often much more sympathetic and understanding than billeting officers. They also ran canteens at arrival points and organised the collection of bedding, clothing and supplies of all kinds. Often, too, they acted as liaison between the children and their parents back in London and helped overcome many emotional problems.

Top: It was not only human beings who left London. Vast piles of important government documents were taken off to safer places. The same thing happened to works of art. The most precious contents of the museums were spread far and wide over the country. The best of the National Gallery paintings were buried deep in a quarry near Blaenau Festiniog, Eros found a home at Egham. Private owners of large valuables, such as furniture, rather than run the risk of having them destroyed in London, lent them to friends in the country for the duration.

Bottom: Among large organisations evacuated to the country was the Hearts of Oak Benefit Society, which moved two hundred and fifty of their people down to Hurstmonceux Castle in Sussex. It is never pleasant to be compulsorily uprooted from your home but in this case there were compensations. The castle is a beautiful place, with ancient lawns and yew trees, roses and cloisters, and it certainly made a change to have your lunch in a baronial hall instead of a pub or cafe. But sorting out thousands of filing cabinets and ledgers brought from London was quite a task.

The lights go out

At the outbreak of war, easily the biggest inconvenience for Londoners generally was the blackout. As night fell, every home had to be blacked out completely so that not a chink or glimmer of light shone out into the street. Ordinary curtains were not enough. Only the very thickest would do. Otherwise extra blackout curtains or screens had to be fixed up every night.

Pubs had to arrange a special light trap—a double door or curtain that would prevent the light escaping as people went in or out. 'That brief flash of light may not seem much to look at' an official of the Ministry of Home Security told journalists, 'but remember, there are five thousand public houses and hotels in London and if someone goes in and out every five minutes there is a constant twinkle of lights.'

Car-owners were advised to use their cars as little as pos-

Boadicea in her chariot by moonlight seemed far more dramatic than under ordinary street lighting. Dramatic, yet somehow unreal, as did so much else in London. If you walked along the Embankment, its lights all out, and saw the moonlight reflected in the river you felt you were in a dream world. An illusion broken perhaps as a convoy of civil defence workers, wardens, firemen, ambulances and the rest, went rumbling by on a night exercise.

sible after dark and, if they did so, had to put cardboard discs with tiny slits in their lamps, so that only the smallest light shone through. Rear lamps had to be stuffed with tissue paper to reduce the intensity of their beam. There were no street lights, of course, and traffic light signals were completely blacked out except for small crosses of red, amber and green. It was hardly surprising, therefore, that during the first ten days of blackout the numbers killed in road accidents in London was nearly five times as great as in the preceding ten days.

Pedestrian torches were also supposed to be stuffed with paper and always pointed in a downward direction—though some shone them on the front of buses in the effort to read their numbers or destinations and sometimes dazzled the drivers. The proper way to stop a bus, according to the Ministry of Information, was to keep your torch pointed down at your feet and switch the light on and off once or twice. Ingenious, perhaps, but it still did not tell you whether the bus you were stopping was the one you wanted to get on. To prevent being bumped into by other people out walking, it was a good idea to smoke or, at least, carry a lighted cigarette. One lady was reported to have been seen in the Upper Richmond Road with a tiny red electric rear-lamp fixed to her belt.

To help lighten the darkness and reduce accidents vast quantities of white paint were used—on kerbs, lamp-posts, sandbags, for example—and miles of white lines appeared on streets that had never seen them before. Some motorists recklessly drove along the lines in their endeavour to find the way.

At first the blackout was accepted as a necessary evil. Then, when there were no raids, everybody began to grumble about it and say it was ridiculous and much too severe. After several months there was some relaxation—for example, inside buses, where you could now, at a pinch, see to read your paper —and before Christmas modified street lighting appeared in some West End streets. All the same, London remained a very dark city and the popular song 'I'll be lit up when the lights go up in London' well expressed what people already felt during those first months.

One interesting social effect was that since travelling after dark was so unpleasant you got to know your immediate neighbours better. Instead of driving a mile or two, or getting on a bus, to look up friends in another district, you tended to stay near your own home. In effect, London after dark reverted to being a number of separate villages. Everybody had their own blackout tales to tell, just as later everybody had their own bomb stories. And, of course, there were innumerable jokes on the subject, including Pont's drawing in 'Punch' of two men in darkness about to walk down a large manhole, with one saying to the other: 'Gosh! Aren't you sick and tired of all these jokes about the blackout?'

Right: Uncounted miles of black paper and cloth were used to make screens and curtains. Putting up the blackout as night approached was a chore everybody hated. In November—the third month of the war—seventy per cent of Mass Observation's national panel were spending five minutes or more each evening doing this little job. Lampshades, especially in the hall, were often shrouded in black paper and even then, before opening the front door, you were advised to turn out the light. Blackout screens were particularly unpleasant in hot weather, since they usually made it impossible to open windows.

Left: Perhaps the people who loathed the blackout most were those who lived in the suburbs and had a long journey home. A doctor wrote a letter to 'The Daily Telegraph' arguing that the lack of light in railway carriages was really rather a good thing, since it helped to relax tension and so had a beneficial effect on travellers' health – 'some go to sleep, others perhaps for the first time in their busy lives have acquired the habit of thinking'. He may have been right but most people soon got heartily sick of darkened buses and trains, where in the early days of the war, until the restrictions were modified, you could not even see who was sitting opposite. They longed for the time when once again there would be a welcoming light in the hall when they got home.

Bottom left: All the same, there were times when London seemed more beautiful than ever before. At sunset or twilight marvellous silhouettes appeared against the sky. And not only at show places, like Westminster. Ordinary buildings one would normally not have looked at twice, reduced to two dimensions sometimes looked quite splendid.

For those with imagination there were, indeed, many compensations, and after dark the Inns of Court or St James's Palace, for example, became wildly romantic.

Below: 'Wear something white' – that was the general advice to people going out in the blackout. So there was quite a run on white coats and macintoshes, white fur, white armbands and, as shown here, white bands for gentlemen's hats. You could even get complete white covers for bowlers. Carrying a white object was also recommended. Women, therefore, bought white handbags, men painted walking sticks, and everybody made a point of carrying newspapers, even when they had finished reading them.

For the first time, if you had lived in London all your life, you got a chance to enjoy the night sky. Without artificial lights you could really see the stars. Even better were nights when the moon was full, so that you could wander about without bumping into people. London was so quiet, too. Because of petrol rationing and the dangers and tedium of blackout driving, there were very few cars on the road once the rush hours were past. There was, indeed, far more peace in Trafalgar Square then than there is now, with the blaze of street lamps and the roar of traffic.

All kinds of people in all kinds of jobs became part-time wardens. This character—obviously the right type—combined his air-raid duties with being a milk roundsman. There were others of a more officious nature who took on the job largely because they enjoyed bossing other people about. Naturally, these were resented. A frequent cause of trouble was the blackout. An eagle-eyed warden would complain about blackout devices already approved by a less fanatical policeman, and the shout 'Put out that light' was not always necessary.

Civil Defence

As early as 1933, when Hitler gained power in Germany, people with foresight here realised air raid precautions might have to be taken. But it was not until 1937 that civil defence really got going—under the control of the local boroughs. That was when the first wardens were enrolled.

In general terms a warden was supposed to consider himself 'a leader of his fellow citizens and, with them and for them, to do the right thing in an emergency.' His duties included patrolling streets during raids and reporting bomb damage; educating his neighbours in how to deal with incendiary bombs; checking to ensure their gasmasks were in good order; giving warning of gas attack; seeing that the blackout was observed. This last was relatively easy so far as the front of houses was concerned, but often harder in regard to the back.

Each warden belonged to a wardens' post manned by from three to six people and responsible for an area with about five hundred inhabitants. The post was connected by telephone to the control centre—usually the town hall. Sometimes there was a messenger service as well, in case telephones got damaged. In reporting 'incidents', wardens were trained to give their estimate of the nature of the damage done and the sort of assistance required so that fire appliances, ambulances, rescue units or whatever could be dispatched with the minimum of delay.

At the start of the war all sorts of people became wardens. Some were paid full-time workers, others volunteer part-timers. Many who normally spent their days sitting at desks got sore feet patrolling London's pavements and were grateful to the British Association of Chiropodists, which offered free treat-

Left: Many women served as wardens—and not only in the capacity of telephonists. When the Blitz came they showed as much stamina and courage as men, not only doing their specific warden's job but also in helping other civil defence services—rescue parties, ambulance services and the rest. Wardens were trained not to panic but always to make their messages back to control as explicit as possible. Thus, the right help could be given without delay or waste of resources.

Below: Wardens were expected to be knowledgeable about a whole host of subjects from first-aid and ambulance work to a rudimentary understanding of building (so that they could tell, for example, whether a damaged house should be evacuated or not). One of the trickier subjects was learning about the different types of gas that might be used—lung irritants, tear gases, sneezing gases, blister gases—and their various smells: floor polish, geraniums, peardrops and so on. Here is a group of wardens attending a lecture in Holborn Town Hall.

Another part of the warden's job was to remind people to keep buckets of sand and water ready to deal with fires started by incendiary bombs. Quick action as soon as the bombs fell might save a whole block of houses or flats. Roofs, of course, were where the fires were likeliest to start, so it was important householders should clear out their lofts and make access to them as easy as possible. Wardens trained groups of neighbours in fire-fighting drill, ready to go into action at a moment's notice. Naturally, people were only too ready to co-operate when, by doing so, they might save their homes going up in flames.

ment at the foot hospital, Rochester Row, Westminster.

Before the war, Londoners as a whole were more fearful of high explosive or gas attacks than of incendiaries. The authorities, however, realised that the main danger might well come from fire. For two years, therefore, the Auxiliary Fire Service had been training men, and when war broke out these and an army of new recruits became full-time firemen.

All through that hot September, thousands of Londoners in full fire-fighting kit, sometimes in gas-kit as well, ran out endless miles of hose and squirted countless gallons of water, training themselves to face the Blitz when it came. Men who had never climbed a ladder before practised carrying their mates from upstairs windows; hairdressers and greengrocers learnt how to make their way through smoke-filled rooms; actors and poets took courses in hydraulics. Like the wardens, the AFS included part-timers as well as full-time members. Enthusiasts would commit themselves, say, to sleeping three nights a week at the fire station, ready to man a pump at once, if required.

There were, of course, other specialised services standing by for action. Decontamination squads; repair services for gas, electricity and water; ambulance services. All these were keyed up, ready to go, on 3 September and then for a year were not needed—for war purposes any way. Happily, the turn of the decontamination squads never came at all.

Morale among the civil defence workers was probably higher than among the public generally. Those enrolled were heartened by the thought that if the bombs fell they would at least have a definite job to do.

Far right: One of the warden's most important responsibilities was to make sure all the people on his beat read and thoroughly understood the basic air-raid precautions. It was no good waiting till the bombs fell before they started to learn what to do. So many wardens went from house to house to check that people really did their homework. It was also a good way to find which of the neighbours were likely to be able to help in an emergency and who were the ones—old people, for example—who might need special assistance.

Right: In the event of gas, it was the warden's job to go round, sounding a rattle. Afterwards, when the streets were safe, he was supposed to ring a hand-bell. Fortunately for the wardens—and everybody else—gas bombs were never dropped.

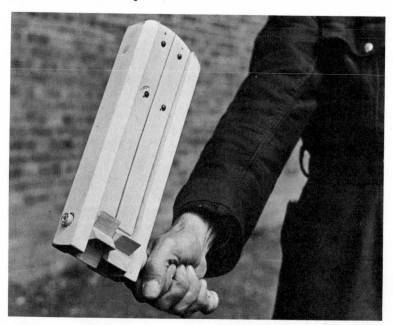

Top left: First job at a fire—or exercise—was to unhitch the trailer pump, drop the chocks and connect it with a hydrant or static water supply. In addition to the river and other natural resources, large tanks of water were put up all over London in case the pipes were bombed. Working from a hydrant was easy enough: the other required more expertise—especially when it might mean relaying water from one pump to another over long distances. The pump man may have had special responsibilities, but it was more fun being on the branch, actually squirting the water on the fire.

Top centre: Most auxiliary firemen were billeted at schools, church halls or other accommodation requisitioned for the purpose. Others joined the regulars at London's peacetime fire stations. Wherever they were, they had to move the second the bells went down. At the regular fire stations they just slipped down the pole to their machines. At the others it might mean fifty yards run or more. Boots, tin hat, axe, belt and gas-mask were kept on, or by, the pump. The volunteer firemen were ready enough to practice fire-fighting but often resented squad drill and cleaning brass.

Bottom left: Learning to crawl through smoke, wearing breathing apparatus was one of the jobs the firemen had to learn. Smoke, of course, rises, so the lower you get the better. Hook ladder drill was another part of the training. You put a ladder with a large hook on it through a first floor window, climbed the ladder, then, sitting astride the sill, lifted the ladder and put it through the window above, climbed it and so on up as many storeys as the instructor thought fit. Most amateurs preferred an ordinary extension ladder or escape.

Left: When war broke out 3,000 of London's 8,000 taxis were requisitioned to draw trailer pumps and many of their drivers went with them into the fire service. They, of course, were only one group. The A.F.S. (later to become the N.F.S.—National Fire Service) was, like the rest of civil defence drawn from all sections of the community. Many of those used to sedentary lives, with routine office jobs, found it refreshing to be doing something which required more physical exertion. They felt better for losing weight. And, for some at any rate, it was a relief to have, so long as there was a risk of raids, guaranteed employment.

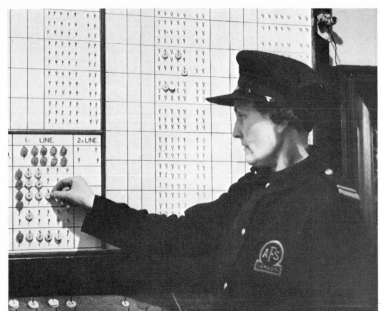

Left: Women in the fire service were generally employed as telephonists or in control rooms, to keep tabs on the whereabouts of pumps during fires and exercises. In the early months of the war it was not an arduous job, but when the raids came it called for a cool head and plenty of common sense. With fires raging in all directions and the demand for pumps exceeding those available, it was vitally important for officers to know exactly what strength they had to hand at any moment. At the height of the Blitz A.F.S. girls also drove canteens to the men at the fires.

Bottom left: Firemen, like wardens, also spent time training the public how to use stirrup pumps to protect their homes the moment incendiaries fell, before the fires got really going. The pump, which worked like an old-fashioned tyre pump, was attached to thirty feet of half-inch hose. It was a three-man drill. One held the nozzle, the second did the pumping, the third brought

fresh supplies of water. The nozzle had two positions—spray for the bomb, jet for the fire—and you were trained, when holding it, to lie down, since in a real emergency you would most likely have to use it in a smoke-filled room or loft, where the clearer air would be close to the ground.

Below: You could identify the various civil defence services by the letters on their helmets. You cannot see the letter on this one but, in fact, it was 'R'—'R' for Rescue. It was the job of the rescue squads to clear away debris and get the people out of bombed buildings. Other letters on hats were: RP/R (Repair Service—Roads). RP/G (Repair Service—Gas), RP/E (Repair Service—Electricity), RP/W (Repair Service—Water). Exercises were carried out in mobilising all these services, but it was only after the bombs fell in 1940 that anyone could fully realise what the work entailed.

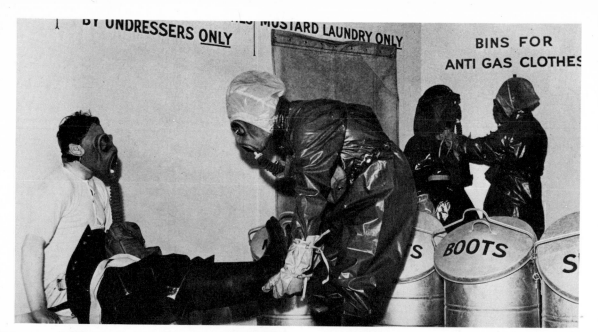

Top left: Special decontamination squads were organised to clean the streets after gas had been used. Doing heavy work in full anti-gas kit, through which air could not penetrate, was a sweaty and exhausting experience, and only the toughest could stand up to it for long. Even if it had only been a rehearsal—for something which, as it turned out, was never going to happen— it was always a relief to be stripped and feel fresh air round your body again. Large steam boilers were ready to clean the anti-gas kit.

Bottom left: Here is a rescue squad off on a training exercise in Holborn. Civil defence exercises of all kinds—sometimes combining the various branches of the service—could be interesting and enjoyable enough if the weather was fine and those in charge gave proper explanations—either while the exercise was on or afterwards. As winter drew on, however, and the novelty wore off exercises often became something of a bore. Not that anyone looked forward to the real thing—which, apart from anything else, might mean the destruction of home and family.

Top right: As well as the army of civil defence workers, auxiliary police were enrolled to help the regulars in many of their duties. The extra police would have been especially valuable if the war had started with heavy bombing, leading to panic. As it was, they played a substantial part in reducing crime— which inevitably flourished in war conditions (though, oddly enough, during the first two months of the blackout declined, quickly to rise again). Quite a number of celebrities—including famous sportsmen join the police—including the Compton brothers.

Bottom right: Round about the time of Munich a group of yachtsmen, boat-builders and others who liked 'mucking about in boats' formed a River Emergency Service, to give whatever help they could on the Thames during air raids. These were all amateurs, notable among them A.P. Herbert. In 1940, when there was the possibility of invasion, they were merged in the Royal Naval Patrol Service and their responsibilities extended. Part of their duty now was to challenge all craft coming up river to ensure there were no unwanted visitors.

Right and below: Ambulance girls, like the rest of the A.R.P. workers, had to be ready to do their job even if gas bombs had been dropped—so some of their training was done in anti-gas kit. In this rehearsal—since the ladies have removed their gas-masks—the assumption appears to be that the worst of the attack is over. This assumption was often made at civil defence exercises—especially in hot weather, when working in a gas-mask as well as tin hat and anti-gas clothing was almost unbearable.

Far right: The patient has now received first-aid, on-the-spot treatment and is being carried to the ambulance. When men did the job, it was usually four to a stretcher but for women the regulation number was six. Everyone was dedicated to the job and took the training seriously—after all, when it came to the point, it was often going to be a matter of life and death but, naturally enough, at rehearsals there was often plenty of laughter when the instructor was looking the other way.

Top left: By mid-September there were five thousand ambulance drivers and attendants, standing ready at a hundred and ten posts throughout London. At least a third of these were women in their twenties. They had to be expert drivers and were trained to drive heavy vehicles even in the blackout. They also had to have at least a rudimentary knowledge of first aid. They were paid two pounds a week and worked all round the clock in eight-hour shifts, the girls on night duty sometimes sleeping in the garage next to their ambulance. They got one day off a week.

Bottom left: Here is a group of nurses arriving at a clearing station. These particular ladies were fully trained members of St John Ambulance Brigade. London was lucky to be able to call on women with such experience and devotion to humanitarian work. They formed an elite, able to guide and help the many new volunteer nurses, eager to do their best but not always knowing a great deal about how to go about it. When the testing time came, it was often found that the older women had more stamina than their juniors.

Right: This is the sort of thing ambulance drivers saw when they got their casualties to hospital. It was not only the ambulance drivers who saw it. Such notices brought home to hundreds of thousands on their way to and from work that they and their families might at any time now be stretcher cases. To many, the stark words CASUALTY CLEARING STATION stuck up in a familiar London street brought home the ugly possibilities of the war more vividly than anything else. They remembered seeing the words before—only that time it had been in France, in World War One.

Top: In the years before the war, when A.R.P. was being developed, it became obvious that if the bombs ever dropped, London's hospitals would be hopelessly inadequate to deal with all the casualties. Some attempt had, therefore, been made to increase accommodation—the basement of the Old Bailey, for example, had been made an annexe to Guy's—and at the outbreak patients who could easily be moved were sent either home or to hospitals in the country. Five days after war was declared the Prime Minister stated in the House of Commons that in London there were 56,000 beds ready for air-raid cases. The nurses in this picture were preparing for casualties at Queen Alexandra's Military Hospital, Millbank.

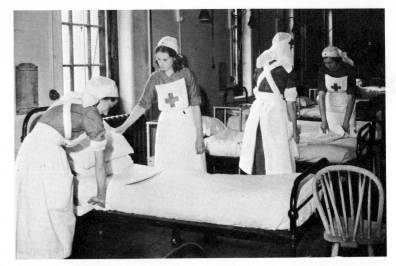

Centre: By the end of the first week, over fifty thousand auxiliary nurses had joined the Civil Nurses Reserve for service to hospitals and first aid posts, and nearly two thousand five hundred doctors had accepted enrolment in the Emergency Medical Service. The biggest enrolment was, understandably, in London and the doctors included men who would normally have been seeing wealthy patients in Harley Street. It was realised that surgeons might have to operate in gas-contaminated areas, so doctors sometimes attended rehearsals wearing gas-masks.

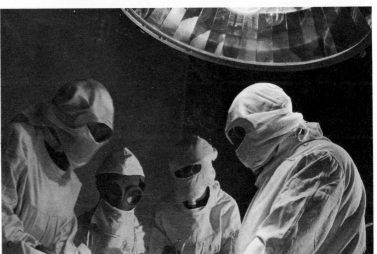

Bottom: It was a sad time for London's dogs and cats. In September 1939 there were long, miserable queues outside all the vets, with owners taking their pets to be put down. Some of these were people leaving London who could not—or did not want to—take animals to their new homes. Others who felt that dogs, in particular, would suffer too much from the noise of the raids apart from anything else. Gas-masks were impracticable for the animals themselves but some animal-lovers practised taking them to gas-proof quarters in the event of a raid.

70

At camps and training grounds round London—as indeed all over Britain—troops were getting used to wearing battle dress. Then the moment came to say goodbye to wives, children, mothers before setting off for France. How soon they would see fighting was anybody's guess but no-one at the time imagined it would be more than six months before they met the Germans in open battle. The first British troops began to land on French soil on September 4th and the first army corps was ashore by September 19th.

After the first excitement

There was no television service during the war but since there had been only about two hundred thousand sets in use throughout the whole country not many Londoners felt deprived. Everybody, however, listened to radio—for the news, if for nothing else. In the earliest days of the war it was news, government announcements, record programmes, Sandy Macpherson at the cinema organ and nothing else. After that, things got livelier. Just before the war ITMA ('Its That Man Again') with Tommie Handley had been tried out and withdrawn, but on 19 September it really got going and for years had the most fantastic success with all sections of the public. Other favourite radio shows were 'Band Waggon' with Arthur Askey and Richard Murdoch and 'Garrison Theatre' with Jack Warner.

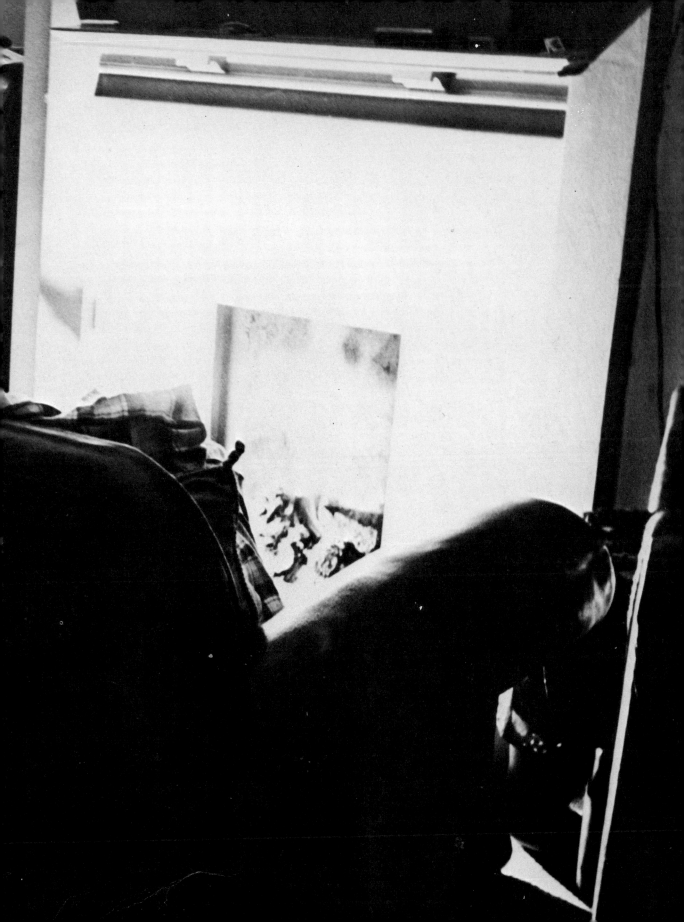

As late summer gave way to Autumn the mood in London changed. After the tension of the first days in September there was a sense of anti-climax. It was not just that there had been no raids on London. There was no fighting in Western Europe at all. Our planes had certainly dropped propaganda leaflets over Germany and the war at sea was real enough—on the very first night of the war the passenger liner, Athenia, had been torpedoed—but so far as ordinary homes in Hackney or Hammersmith, Brixton or Bethnal Green were concerned, unless the menfolk were away on active service, the whole thing seemed rather remote.

People of intelligence and resolution knew this was only a lull before the storm. But there were others, either because they were simple or, for one reason or another, anti-war, who argued that since we had failed to stop the Germans and Russians from over-running Poland, perhaps Mr Chamberlain might make yet another deal with Hitler and restore peace. This, too, was of course Hitler's hope. There was also a lot of wishful thinking on the lines that we could in time win the war simply by means of blockade. By preventing Germany from getting oil and other vital supplies we could bring her war effort to a halt more or less without bloodshed.

After the first few weeks, when not a single enemy plane had appeared over England, Londoners felt they might as well return to something more like normal living conditions. Very soon the children began to trickle back from the country and soon the trickle became a stream. Many had been so unhappy in their billets that their parents swore that, come what may, they would not have them evacuated again. In many cases they held to this decision and the following year, when the Blitz began, kept their families together even when their homes were burnt to the ground. One trouble was that the teachers had gone with the evacuees and the vast majority of London schools were closed (even well into the spring of 1940 less than a third had re-opened) so many children spent much of the time running wild.

As the nights grew longer the blackout became harder to bear and became increasingly a cause for grumbling. People back from Paris—quite a few were still taking late holidays abroad—reported that restrictions there were nothing like so severe and asked why we could not copy the French? In any case, it was argued, if Hitler had intended to bomb London he would have done it right at the start when we were only half ready. He would not have waited till now.

ARP workers also came in for a good deal of criticism. When war broke out the wardens were popular enough. Most people were glad to know there was one man in the street, at least, who was supposed to know what to do in an air-raid. But as the weeks went by and the raiders did not come, public

Right: Behind the blackout curtains everything could still be very cosy. With less temptation to go out, people settled down with books they had always meant to read but somehow never got around to—great solid works like Gibbon's 'Decline and Fall' or Carlyle's 'French Revolution'. There was a big demand for Penguin Specials, price only 6d, dealing with recent history and current affairs, such as 'Germany Puts the Clock Back' by Edgar Mowrer. There was also a demand for Jane Austen and Trollope who took you as far away from Hitler and the Nazis as possible.

opinion became less favourable. Amateur part-time wardens—the great majority—might be all very well, but what were the authorities doing handing out the rate-payers' money to thousands of men who, so far as the ordinary citizen could see, appeared to be having a pretty cushy time of it? According to some people, the wardens spent most of their time playing darts or brewing tea. Another thing that irked motorists—at a time of strict petrol rationing—was to see fleets of civil defence vehicles off to imaginary 'incidents'. 'Grown men playing like kids' was a frequent comment—especially when obviously healthy citizens were acting as casualties.

For many, indeed, winter 1939—40 wasn't so very different from the last one. They still had the same jobs and homes, the same entertainments and hobbies. Even football pools got going again in a unified system. It was not really war. It was not really peace. And for Londoners things remained very much the same right on into the spring.

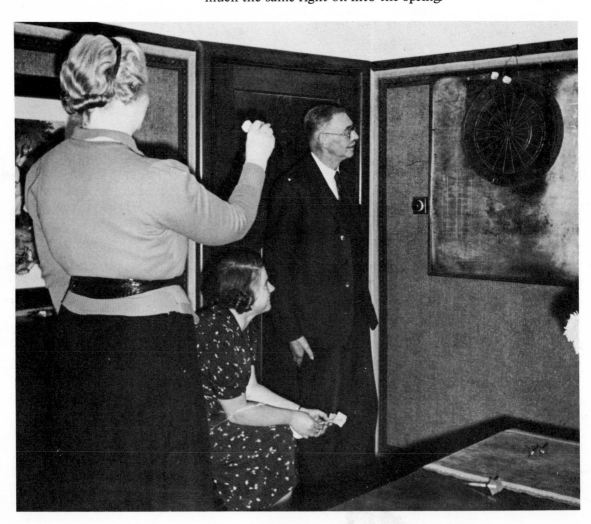

Bottom left: You did not have to go out for a game of darts, either. To save stumbling through the pitch-dark streets or using up precious petrol coupons, more and more people bought their own dart boards. And for company you could always ask in the neighbours. In the new circumstances in which many found themselves with grown up children away in the services and young children and grandchildren still evacuated they were readier than usual to make new friends. In any case, A.R.P. had drawn people together, so it was silly to pretend you did not know the people next door.

Below: Soldiers on leave, your own family and friends or simply boys billeted near by, livened things up, of course, and maybe gave you the chance of a singsong. 'There'll Always Be An England' was a new song and had a great vogue but among the younger generation, at any rate, 'Knees Up Mother Brown' was probably more popular:

'Joe brought his concertina
  and Nobby brought his beer,
And all the little nippers
  swung on the chandelier!
A blackout warden, passing,
  yelled, 'Ma, pull down that blind;
Just look at what you're showin'
  and we shouted 'Never mind!'

Knees up, Mother Brown!
Well, knees up, Mother Brown!
Come along, dearie, let it go;
Ee-i, ee-i, ee-i, oh!
It's yer bloomin' birthday;
  let's wake up all the town!
So knees up, knees up,
  don't get the breeze up,
Knees up, Mother Brown!'

Left: The model-makers certainly had plenty of new ideas to think about and long before Christmas the shops were full of wonderful new toys—clockwork balloon barrages, bren gun carriers and the latest types of tank. Dolls—plentiful as ever—had smart-looking gas-mask carriers slung across their shoulders and, of course, many were dressed as nurses or members of the armed or civil defence services. For children's fancy dress, too, the great thing was to have tin hats with letters to represent wardens, rescue or ambulance, according to taste.

Bottom left: As in World War One, there was a great craze for knitting. This time the scarves and socks, gloves, pullovers and balaclava helmets were not only for soldiers, sailors and airmen, but also for the thousands of civil defence personnel standing by on cold nights in London. The winter turned out to be

an exceptionally bitter one but, quite apart from the weather, many wardens, auxiliary firemen and the rest, accustomed to sedentary jobs, realised for the first time what a difference it made having good, thick, hand-knitted socks, when you were on your feet for hours on end.

Below right: A useful way of passing the dark evenings was to practise first aid. In some streets wardens organised special first-aid classes, where doctors and nurses gave professional training. Pretending to be a casualty may not have been the most exciting way of spending your spare time, but a year later the lives of many Londoners crushed by falling houses or torn by splintered glass were saved by the prompt and skilful action of those who had learnt the right thing to do during the months they waited.

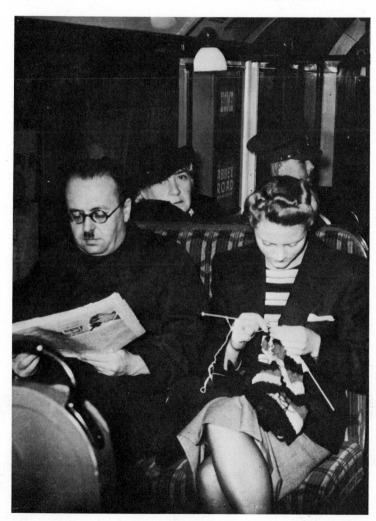

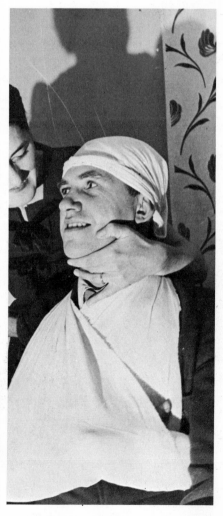

Below: Knitting went on everywhere. In addition to regular knitting parties organised by churches and women's guilds, all sorts of publicity stunts were arranged to give encouragement. Photographs appeared in the Press of the chorus girls at the Windmill knitting, of page boys at the Dorchester doing the same. If you were driving out of London and stopped at 'The Peggy Bedford', pictured here, the landlady might ask you to do a few rows for soldiers or evacuated children while you drank your pint.

Right: Even old gentlemen who remembered the Boer War, let alone the 1914– 18 affair, got to work with the needles, though they may have had to be helped with the casting on and may on occasion have dropped a stitch without being able to find it. This particular knitter lived at Harmondsworth, near London's airport.

Bottom left: Soon after the outbreak, Eros disappeared from Piccadilly Circus —evacuated to Egham—and, for a time, this seemed to symbolise the loss of gaiety in the West End. But long before Christmas things had brightened up and the entertainment world was booming. Note in the picture the posters for National War Bonds and just below them women with their flower baskets. (There were always flower women there before the war, so why should they move for Hitler?) Note, too, the sign about public shelters in Lower Regent Street and the white paint on kerbs, lamp posts and taxis.

Right: You could still enjoy marvellous meals in London, provided you had the money. Food rationing did not start till 1940, and even then it was a considerable time before it seriously affected good restaurants, but prices were going up. Large imports of all kinds of luxury foods and wines continued to arrive from France and nobody talked much yet of austerity. Supplies of hock were running down but who wanted to drink German wine any way? The biggest change in restaurants was in the clientele—far more people now in uniform.

Bottom right: There were many soldiers in London, passing through on their way to France. Away from their own girl friends, these were especially glad to find places where partners were laid on. It was the same with troops from the Dominions and later from the United States. Army boots were not ideal for dancing, particularly if you trod on your partner's feet, but these girls, no doubt, could look after themselves. Perhaps they were just going to try the new dance, 'The Blackout Stroll', during which the lights went out while you changed partners:

'There's no more cuddling
  in the moonlight,
There's no more petting in the park.
But why let's worry over moonlight?
For when we're strolling in the dark
  IT'S LOVELY.
Everybody do 'The Blackout Stroll',
Laugh and drive your cares right up
  the pole,
Whisper 'see ya later' to your baby doll,
For now we change our partners in
  'The Blackout Stroll'.

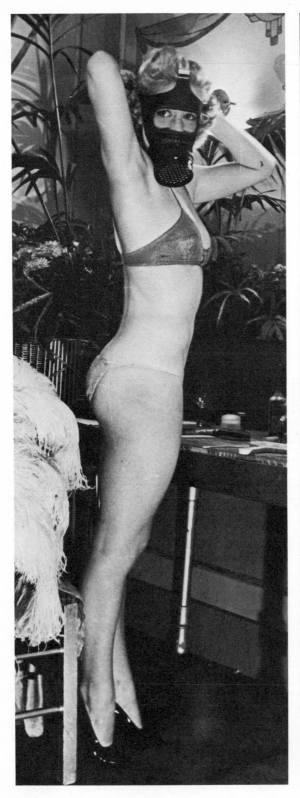

Far left: Gas-mask drill? Hardly. London press photographers during the war still retained the knack of cooking up a crazy, eye-stopping picture.

Left: At some night clubs, like the Paradise, you knew you would be safe even in a raid—though dancing, rather than raids, was in people's thoughts that winter. Ed Murrow, in one of his famous broadcasts to America, said on 16 November: 'There are more dance bands playing in the West End now than in the months before peace went underground. Any establishments where we could eat in those old days have now engaged small orchestras. Customers want to dance. Places like the Embassy Club, Quaglinos, the Paradise, Cafe de Paris are jammed nearly every night. People come early and stay late ... practically no-one wears formal evening dress. That's a change from pre-war days.'

Below: During the first weeks all night clubs and dance halls were closed but it was not long before the crowds were bigger than ever. Partly, no doubt, it was due to the blackout. Young people who might normally have been roaming about the streets, looking in shop windows, wanted to go somewhere bright and cheerful. For dance bands, in particular it was a wonderful time—Joe Loss said the biggest boom in his experience. New Year's Eve celebrations were in the best peacetime tradition. At the Savoy there were three cabarets, with the trumpeters of the Life Guards to welcome the New Year; similar attractions at the Berkeley; and at more modest prices you got gala entertainment at the Regent or Strand Palace or Lyons Corner Houses.

Above: For those who wanted wit, there was Herbert Farjeon's 'Little Revue', starring Hermione Baddeley. (The Little Theatre in the Adelphi, where it was staged, was destroyed by bombs in April 1941). As for balletomanes, they could see four separate companies at four separate theatres. In fact, the total number of theatres open in London that Christmas was larger than the year before. Many of the audiences were, of course, swollen by troops home on leave.

Above right: Such a thing could hardly have happened in World War I—a major fraternising with a Tommy in a West End night club. But this time, all ranks from generals to privates could be found in the smartest places mixing with all kinds of other uniformed characters, particularly women—Ats, Waafs, Wrens, Firewomen and so on. The war did a tremendous amount to break down class distinction. In Autumn 1940 during the Blitz the trend was accelerated—when people were being mutilated and killed their accents hardly seemed to matter. But even before that the divisions were becoming less rigid.

Right: Another place to go to forget about the blackout was Collin's Music Hall, Islington. This was always a great place for cockneys. In the intervals, it was part of the tradition, as illustrated here, for the artists to go round and have a chat with patrons in the promenade bars. Another music hall, on a much grander scale, was the Holborn Empire where the big attraction was Max Miller, at this time starring in a show called 'Haw-Haw' (the name given to William Joyce, who used to broadcast from Germany, trying to undermine British morale). The Holborn Empire was a victim of the Blitz in May 1941. Collin's survived until a fire in 1958.

For soldiers on leave that Christmas one of the big attractions was the leg show at the Prince of Wales's Theatre, though the seat prices were a bit steep. There were plenty of other big shows to choose from, too. Jack Hulbert and Cecily Courtnedge were at the Palace, Lupino Lane was doing the Lambeth Walk in 'Me and My Girl' and there was pantomime at the Coliseum. Or, if you preferred straight plays, Gielgud, Edith Evans and Peggy Ashcroft were in 'The Importance of Being Earnest'; Sybil Thorndike and Emlyn Williams in 'The Corn is Green'; Godfrey Tearle in Julius Caesar'.

PRINCE OF WALES THEATRE

NO MONEY REFUNDED

NO RE-ADMISSION

OPEN TILL 10 P.

PRICES of ADMISSION
STALLS and CIRCLE
IF AVAILABLE

2'6   3'6   4'6

6'-   8'6   10'6

SEATS BOOKABLE IN ADVANCE

6'-   8'6   10'6

ALL INCLUDING TAX •

SPECIAL TERMS
— FOR PARTIES OF OVER TWENTY

DON'T HELP
THE ENEMY!

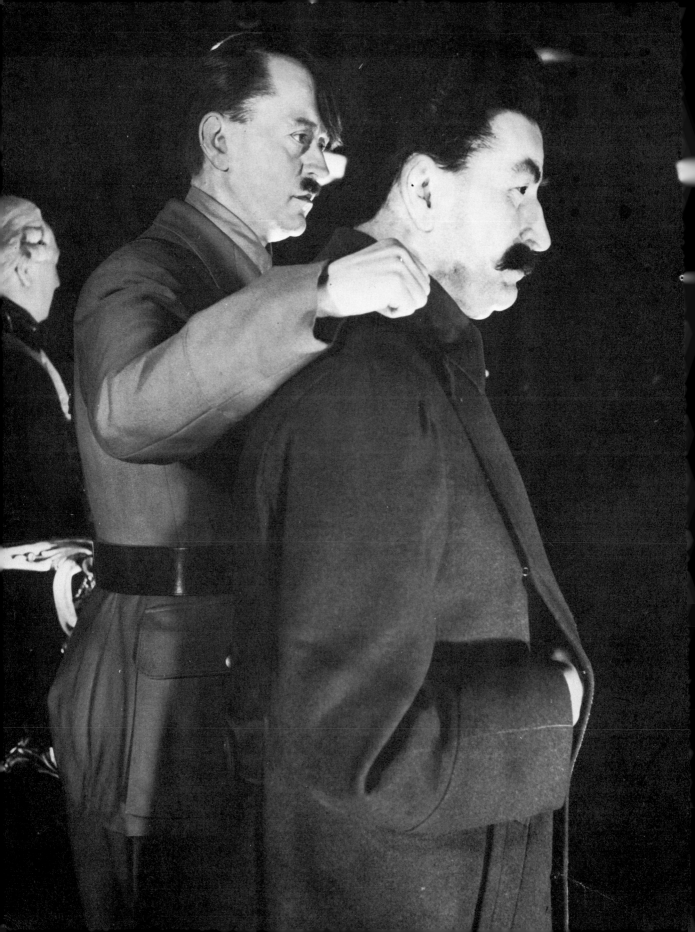

Left: You could also drop in at Madame Tussaud's and have a look at Hitler resting a brotherly hand on Stalin's shoulder. The German-Soviet pact of August had been a frightful blow for the British public. For years Nazis and Communists had been screaming abuse at each other for all they were worth and, while that was going on, there had always been the hope that if we got involved in a war with Hitler, Stalin might take the opportunity of attacking the eastern frontier. But when the pact was signed that hope was gone .and there was a gloomy fascination in seeing the dictators shoulder to shoulder. Tussaud's, too,

got a bomb early in September 1940.
Below: Among the famous innovations of the early war months were the lunch-time concerts at the National Gallery organised by Myra Hess. At the first of these an audience of a thousand turned up to hear her play Scarlatti, Bach and the Appassionata Sonata. People sometimes ate sandwiches while they sat on the floor and listened. In this picture the young Eileen Joyce sits in the foreground. For many young people it was their first introduction to classical music. A few pictures hung on the walls but the valuable ones had all been removed to safety.

Far left: The fashion houses continued to flourish. This white dinner dress in silk jersey, with a spray of pearls at the waist—from Hartnell's spring collection, 1940—shows that despite the war, women in London could still be elegant enough. Right up to the fall of France and the threat of invasion there were very few deprivations for the rich.

Left: All kinds of attractive siren suits were produced, ready to slip on—especially at night—if there was a raid.

This particular one, with hood attached, was made from gas-proof oil silk and was available in pastel shades with a winceyette lining to match.

Below: Obviously this white wool coat, with hat to match, had been inspired by the trials and tribulations of the blackout. Note, too, the torch in the side of the lady's case—very handy when crossing the road to show when you had arrived at the kerb.

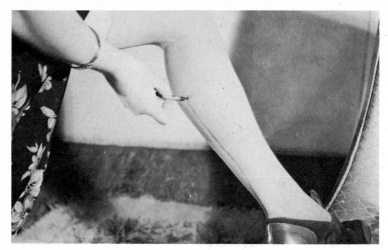

Left: To overcome stocking shortages a leg make-up kit appeared on the market. You smeared a cream, available in four shades, over your legs and then, since it was important to have a seam-line showing, marked it up the back with a dark brown pencil. All right perhaps if you had an exceptionally steady hand or, better still, if your boy friend was an artist. It was claimed that the cream would not come off with rubbing or if you were caught in a shower but only if you applied soap and water.

Below: Trousers, hardly known for women in town before the war, became fashionable. The lady in this picture, exercising her dog round Regent's Park, is Phyllis Robins, at that time playing in 'Shepherd's Pie', a very popular revue at the Prince's.

Left: Happiest London families that Christmas were those with a soldier back from France, like this sergeant staying with his wife at her parents' home in St John's Wood. So far, it had been as safe across the Channel as it had been here. No shells on the French front. No bombs on London. But separation is separation. And who knew what might happen before they met again?

Below: Despite the steady trek back to London, there was still a host of evacuee children who spent that Christmas away from home. This picture shows a little trio, plus toys, at Hutton Residential School, Shenfield, Essex. Those who had stayed away had often by this time adapted themselves to the new environment and were happy enough and, of course, in many cases had been visited by their parents at weekends. All the same, there can be little doubt the vast majority were longing for the time when once again they could be at home with Mum.

Right: Another evacuee at the school at Shenfield. Probably those billeted at schools were the luckiest. Being in your own home is one thing. Being in someone else's quite another. Especially at Christmas time. You might be with someone who did not understand children. Or someone whose own children were not very kind to you. There might not be anywhere for you to play or you might not get the sort of toys you wanted. Most people, it seems likely, gave the children a special treat even if they, like the children themselves, hoped it would be the only time they would spend Christmas together.

Left: Food rationing began in January 1940 with butter restricted to four ounces a week, bacon four ounces, and sugar twelve ounces. Meat did not go on ration till March, when everybody over the age of six was entitled to one and tenpence worth. This did not include 'offal' (kidneys, liver, heart, sweetbreads) so naturally enough there was a heavy demand for these. Tea rationing, which many Londoners—especially old age pensioners—found the hardest to bear, did not come in until July.

Bottom left: In February Londoners had a real break. The biggest crowd since the coronation, nearly three years before, turned out to honour the 760 officers and men of the cruisers Ajax and Exeter. This was at a triumphal march to celebrate the victory over the German battleship Graf Spee. There was tremendous excitement, with wildly cheering men, women and children, and flags and streamers everywhere. The sailors marched from Waterloo to the

Horse Guards, where they were inspected by the King, then on to lunch at the Guildhall. After lunch many of them got the autograph of the First Lord of the Admiralty, obviously at his most exuberant.

Below: In 1940, Easter came early and, after the blackout, was more than usually welcome. There was a big rush out of London. An official at Euston said it was the busiest Good Friday they had known for many years, takings being double what they were accustomed to. And it was much the same at the other big stations, from which heavy extra services were operating. One reason for the rail increase was, of course, petrol rationing, which kept many cars off the road. This particular crowd was at the Happy Valley, Llandudno, listening to a concert party.

Below: Many people went away specially to make up for the holiday they had missed in September when war broke out. The weather was not so warm now but, at any rate, it made a change. Those who stayed in London and visited Hampstead Heath found the fair well up to standard with new attractions as well. There were more games with darts ('Air raid warden off duty' people would say of anyone particularly skilful) and Hitler's head had been added to the coconut shies. Big crowds turned up at Whipsnade and, since you do not need petrol for a bicycle, the roads were full of cyclists.

Right: Few who got away—from London or anywhere else—showed this degree of herosim, but the call of the sea is always strong. Brighton and Southend hotels soon filled up and people were turned away. There were, however, bigger than usual crowds coming into London, too. Civil servants evacuated to Blackpool, for example, decided the best way of spending the weekend was back home in Golders Green or Wimbledon. And other people, who had left London of their own choice, felt it was time to see, if not the city lights, at least the city streets and shops and theatres.

The fighting

Early in April, the war which all the while had continued at sea suddenly flared up again in Europe. This time the flames started in Norway. People in London, as throughout the country, were concerned, of course; but Norway was a long way off and few Londoners at the time related the Norwegian defeat to their own lives. It was quite a different thing when on 10 May they learnt the Nazis had invaded Holland and Belgium. Now, for the first time, this was war as everybody understood it, war with the Germans on their way to France and the Channel, war in which our boys would do the killing and be killed. Everybody expected there would be months, perhaps years, of bloody fighting over the same ground where the last generation had fought.

Instead, unbelievably, in a few short weeks the whole campaign was over. Within days of the German attack, London was receiving Dutch and Belgian refugees from countries completely under Nazi control. Then came Dunkirk. And shortly after that the French surrender.

At Victoria and London's other big stations, there were always soldiers coming and going. Those arriving on leave or going back to France in the early days of May never dreamed what would happen to them before the month was out. So far, the war had been unbelievably quiet—training, digging in, sentry duty, reconnaissance, but nothing you could really call fighting. Something was pretty certain to start up soon but 'Dunkirk' was still only the name of a disembarkation port and the possibility that in four short weeks the B.E.F. would be back in England can never have entered anyone's mind.

comes nearer

There was only one question now: what would Hitler do next? Would he try to terrorise us into submission by bombing London as he had bombed Rotterdam, and as we had expected at the outset? Or would he try invasion? Apparently, the latter. Throughout July and August there were no large-scale raids on London but all-out mass attacks on the RAF and its installations, an essential part of an invasion strategy. Every evening there was only one topic of conversation: 'How many German planes shot down today?' Londoners, who often could see the Spitfires and Hurricanes on their way to battle, read their papers with an avidity they had never known before.

Although the full-scale Blitz on London did not begin until September, there were a number of nuisance raids in the weeks before. Sirens sometimes sounded seven or eight times a day in areas where nothing seemed to happen at all. This raised problems for the authorities. The public had been instructed, on hearing a warning siren, to go to the shelters, but if they were to do this every time, even though no serious raid developed, an enormous number of working hours would be lost in factories engaged in war production and other essentials —all to no purpose. Public opinion was divided as to how seriously the sirens should be taken. A lady from Chelsea, in a letter to a national newspaper, complained about her neighbours, asking if anything could be done to stop them making a noise during air-raids at night. 'I, with several million other Londoners', she wrote, 'stay in my first-floor flat when a raid is in progress and unless I hear bombs or gunfire I do not leave my bed. But my nightly rest is disturbed by the idle chatter of those who go down to the basement every time the sirens sound, and instead of stopping there stand at the open street door and gossip.'

On 14 May, as the German tanks raced towards the Channel and the first possible threat of invasion seemed imminent, Eden had made a radio appeal for men to join a new organisation, the LDV (Local Defence Volunteers), soon to be known by Churchill's much better name: Home Guard. This was a spare-time, unpaid job for British citizens between the ages of 17 and 65, ready to use arms against German invaders of their own particular districts. The appeal was 'chiefly to those in small towns, villages and less densely inhabited suburban areas'. But the response in London was as immediate and wholehearted as anywhere else. Whatever Hitler might do, Londoners would fight back.

'Cheer up! I'll soon be home again!' Saying goodbye after leave was not perhaps so painful as when the soldiers left for France the first time in September. Many had had the odd feeling then that they would be safer in the front line than their wives and children back in London—who might be killed in the devastating air-raids expected. The air-raids might still come even now—there was always the risk when someone as crazy as Hitler was running things—but the chances certainly seemed much less. Many of the wives, too, must have felt that since the Germans had not yet moved in France, perhaps for the time being any way, their husbands were not in so much danger.

Below: For the refugees from Holland and Belgium the government made a central reception area at Wembley Stadium until homes could be found for them. Twenty London boroughs were asked to join in solving this problem. There was a ready response and many people who felt they could not offer a home gave blankets, clothes and bedding. The arrival of the refugees made people more than ever thankful there was the Channel to prevent the Nazi tanks rumbling straight on into England, to make refugees of our own old people and children.

Right: Older Londoners who watched the trains out could not help thinking how different it was from the 1914–18 war. Then, the outgoing troops knew only too well what they were going back to—mud, trenches, barbed wire, shells, bayonets, slaughter. And the incoming trains were heavy with tragedy, laden with sick and dying. A few weeks later, when the troops came back from Dunkirk, there were casualties enough. And bitterness. Determination, too. Determination that, though the Germans had driven us out of Europe this time, sooner or later we should be going back.

Left: So far, there had been just one war disaster. On the last night of April a Heinkel bomber, damaged by gunfire, crashed at Clacton. Two civilians and the four members of the crew were killed at once and there were over a hundred and fifty people injured, many of them seriously so. There was also heavy damage to property for over three quarters of a mile. The plane, it seems, was laying magnetic mines in the Thames Estuary and had been hit by A.A. fire, the mines it still carried causing much of the damage at Clacton. The casualties were the first on English soil since the outbreak of war eight months earlier.

Bottom left: Many of the refugees had terrible stories to tell, not only of shelling and bombing in their own countries but also of machine-gunning from low-flying German planes as they crossed in the boat. Most managed to bring at least one suitcase or bundle, but some had only the clothes in which they stood. English people who could speak French, Dutch or Flemish turned up to give voluntary help at the London stations and reception centres. They could now see for themselves the tragedies war inevitably brings.

Far right: In May when Churchill succeeded Chamberlain as Prime Minister, he appointed as Minister of Supply the son of a Brixton policeman: Herbert Morrison. Morrison had already made a big reputation for himself with Londoners as a highly energetic leader of the LCC. In his new position, he devoted his energy, as he himself put it, to providing 'everything from army blankets

to A.A. guns and tanks'. Part of his job was to get as much material as possible from salvage and so save space on our ships, now under increasingly heavy attack from German U-boats.

Bottom right: For the second time in her life this old lady of eighty-one found herself a refugee from the Germans. She was, not surprisingly, tired when she reached Wembley but her spirit was undaunted. She could still remember the English she had learnt when she was here in World War I. There were some, mothers with babies now, who when they came the first time had themselves been children in arms. It was, of course, to be four long years and more before these people were able to return to their native lands.

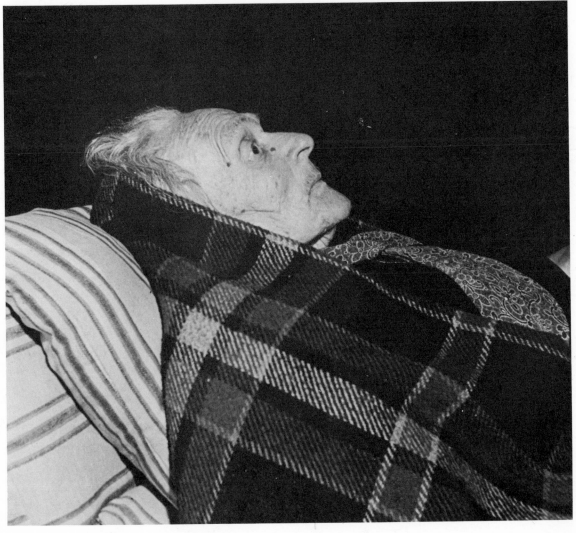

110

Far left: As part of the salvage drive, constant appeals were made to the public to save everything they possibly could and not to throw their waste all together into the same dustbin. A good housewife, doing her bit to win the war, kept at least four separate containers: one for tins and other metal—used for aeroplanes and tanks; one for paper and cardboard—to make food containers for troops, cases for rifles and shells; one for bones to be turned into glue for aeroplanes, glycerine for explosives; and edible waste for feeding pigs. The WVS lady in the picture was a duchess.

Left: Many local councils and dustmen took the salvage drive seriously enough. Some, however, were half-hearted, and it was disappointing after you had taken care to keep your old newspapers carefully separated from your soup tins and bacon rind to see them all shot together into the same dustcart. The Ministry of Information, in an appeal to self-interest as well as patriotism, told the public to put pressure on their councils to be more ardent in salvage collection: 'Much of the material will command a good price when sold to factories and the proceeds will help local authorities to keep down the rates'.

The need, of course, was especially for metal. Everyone was asked to go through their cupboards and lofts and sheds to get rid of everything they did not really want. An enormous amount of junk was produced, as a result, and this was collected and taken to a sorting office, such as this one at Farm Street, Westminster. It looks as though this particular picture must have been taken after the raids on London began—apparently a church had been damaged and a plane shot down—but the salvage drive was well under way before that happened.

Left: Much of the scrap metal went to a depot in Canning Town, where it was sorted. Experienced men could tell at once, by the feel, to which variety of metal a particular piece belonged. Lord Beaverbrook, in charge of aircraft production, was particularly avid for aluminium. 'Everyone' he said, 'who has pots and pans, kettles, vacuum cleaners, hat pegs, coat hangers, shoe trees, bathroom fittings and household ornaments, cigarette boxes, or any other articles made wholly or in part of aluminium, should hand them over at once'. Not all housewives felt they could give up their vacuum cleaners.

Below: There was a good deal of controversy when metal railings were taken up from London squares. Some people argued that quite apart from the need to help the war effort, it was a good thing for the railings to disappear, so that children could play in the gardens. Others, that the gardens belonged to the residents and it was not fair that their property should be thrown open to the general public. They also maintained that the cost of taking up the railings outweighed their value. In this picture the railings are being removed from Marlborough House, home of Queen Mary.

Below: 'Dig for Victory' was one of the famous slogans of the time. At the end of the First World War there had been a million and a half allotments in Britain but by 1939 there were less than a million. However, in only a few months there were a hundred and fifty thousand more. Here are a couple working on their plot in Dulwich. Fulham, too, was a district where there was plenty of enthusiasm. Two of the local vicars set a good example by having their gardens turned into allotments and the Bishop of London did the same with Fulham Palace Meadow.

Right: During 1940, pig clubs became a craze and many were started in and around London, including the Hyde Park police piggery, which produced many an excellent rasher. Hotels and restaurants kept pig buckets, which were collected regularly, to provide the animals with food but, as a government leaflet pointed out, 'pigs should *not* eat orange, lemon, grapefruit or banana skins, rhubarb leaves, egg shells, coffee grounds, tea leaves, fish bones, soda, salt, disinfectants or anything that is acid, sour or mouldy.' So care had to be taken.

In the spring and summer of 1940, wherever you went in London, you were likely to see troops from the Dominions. For many, it was to be their first, and only, visit, so naturally they made the most of it, enjoying all the sights. It was very encouraging for Londoners to have these tough fighting men in their midst—especially after the fall of France. We might 'stand alone' but, after all, if 'we' included the Dominions and Empire there were quite a lot of us. Memories of the First World War were revived. There was talk of Vimy Ridge and Galipoli.

Below: One very noticeable feature of London at this time—especially in the normally prosperous suburbs—was the amount of empty property. Some of the former occupants were in the forces. A great many had evacuated themselves to the country or overseas. Foreign visitors had gone home. In Hampstead, for example, pictured here in May, 1940, it was reckoned that one in eight of the properties throughout the borough was not in use. This meant, among other things that to maintain essential services rates had to be increased for those who remained. Local shopkeepers, too, suffered because of loss of trade.

Right: In the summer of 1940 London was to see women conductors on the buses again. When they had appeared during World War I it was felt to be a revolutionary innovation. This time, although there were jokes about them for the first week or two, they were soon accepted as part of normal life. Just as the war was breaking down barriers between the social classes, so it was doing the same between the sexes. By 1940 Londoners had seen far too many women in uniform of one kind or another to wonder much about this latest development.

Left and below: Petrol rationing had been introduced three weeks after war started. Though obviously necessary, this had led to a good deal of petty crime—stealing and selling coupons, syphoning petrol out of other people's tanks and hoarding it—sometimes in dangerous places. It had also led to a run on bicycles. Towards the end of September it had been pretty well impossible to buy a woman's bicycle in London. Another way of getting round the shortage was to have a gas-producing unit attached to your car. Then you could get your fuel supplies from your coalman. After which, all you had to do was light up. It was claimed that with a ten horse-power car you could do over a hundred miles on one hundredweight of fuel. Not many people, however, ran their cars by this method.

Right: You got no pay as a Home Guardsman. You earned your living in the ordinary way, like this Covent Garden porter, and, like him, did your training in your spare time. Volunteers were told they would be issued with uniforms, but many had to wait a long time for these and attended their early parades in flannels, plus fours or gents' natty suitings, with only an armband to identify them as members of an armed force. In some cases, when the first deliveries of denim overalls came through, the buttons were delivered in separate sacks, so they had to be sewn on by the guardsmen's wives.

Left: The day after Eden broadcast his appeal for LDVs the response was so overwhelming that many London police stations where the men went to register ran out of enrolment forms. Churchill said: 'We shall defend every village, every town, every city ... the vast mass of London itself, fought street by street, could easily devour an entire hostile army, and we would rather see London laid in ashes and ruins than that it should be tamely and abjectly enslaved'. That was the spirit in which the volunteers enrolled. The sentry shown here, at headquarters of the Bow Street company, was a barrister. As can be seen from his armband, LDV had by this time become Home Guard.

Bottom left: Part of the Home Guard training was in how to deal with German parachutists, and the word 'parashot' was much used. This was appropriate enough where there were suitable firearms, but at the beginning there was a distressing shortage and many in Dad's Army had to make do with such wea-

pons as duckguns, duelling pistols and flintlock muskets. However, even before there were enough rifles to go round, every day parties of Londoners went off to Bisley to learn how to shoot straight. Some who had nothing to fire with at all were prepared to do battle with cutlasses and pikes.

Bottom right: Various organisations had their own Home Guard units—factories, power stations, newspaper offices, the BBC and so on. MPs and civil servants prepared to defend Westminster. This group were training outside the Foreign Office. Part of their duty was to patrol at night against possible saboteurs. Until the supply of firearms improved, training was given in the use of the pick handle and cosh. You shoved the pick handle in the enemy's stomach then, as he doubled up, hit him on the head with the cosh. The best coshes were made of rubber tubing filled with lead.

Left: Here three MPs are cleaning sten guns. Left to right: Acting Sergeant Vernon Bartlett, Private Sir Geoffrey Shakespeare and Corporal Gordon Touche. The first MP to join the Home Guard was Josiah Wedgwood, then nearing seventy. He wrote at the time: 'I go on duty tomorrow guarding the Terrace, keeping an eye for swastikaed seaplanes buzzing on to the Thames'. After what the Germans had achieved on the Continent, people felt that anything might happen.

Bottom left: A number of schools specially for training Home Guards were set up in London. The most famous of these was at Osterley Park, under the direction of Tom Wintringham, who had had wide experience of guerilla warfare during the Civil War in Spain. Here they were not only taught how to use weapons, but also how to put up road blocks and smoke screens, and specific tactics for the sort of fighting they must expect if the Germans arrived. They be-

came experts, too, in the manufacture of 'Molotov cocktails', as used by the Finns against the Russians. These, anti-tank weapons, were bottles filled with petrol or paraffin, with an improvised fuse attached.

Below: With the threat of invasion, many parents wanted to send their children overseas and the government set up a Children's Overseas Reception Board to organise this. Offers of hospitality poured in from the Dominions and the USA but even with such generosity and free transport there would obviously be incidental expenses and it seems that most who went came from reasonably comfortable homes. A letter to 'The Times' from the Headmaster of Winchester suggested that parents ought not put pressure on older children to go but rather encourage them to stay and help the community. Here are applicants queuing up for a medical.

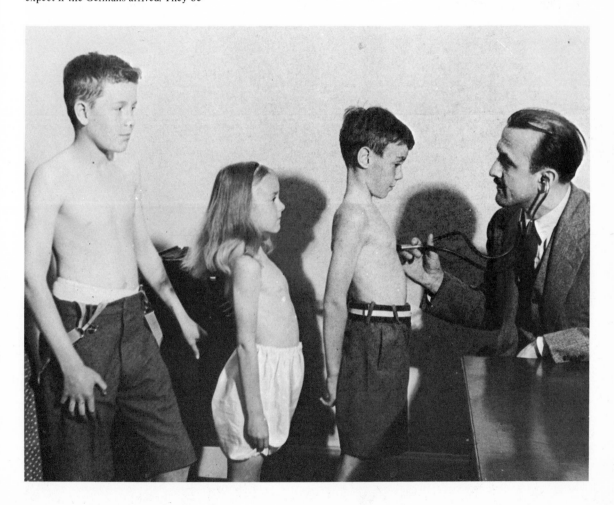

Left: By the time the nuisance raids on London started in August, there were far more public shelters all over London than there had been in the previous autumn. The type shown in this picture was quite common. It gave good protection and was reasonably comfortable for a short time—especially if there were not too many occupants. In the following months, however, during the Blitz, a long night in such conditions was not so cosy—especially if you were not of a gregarious type.

Below: During the Battle of Britain summer, London's favourite resorts on the South and East Coasts were not particularly attractive to holiday makers. Some people went into the country or to the North or West. Others stayed put at home. In Regent's Park, at the Open Air Theatre, they were doing, with gallant irony, 'A Midsummer Night's Dream'. Because of the blackout, evening per-formances started at 6.15 and even then the actors were fading from sight as the play ended. For many it was to be their last memory of a still relatively peaceful London.

Over page: Starting at five o'clock Saturday afternoon, 7 September, for nearly twelve hours, three hundred Nazi bombers, accompanied by six hundred fighters, rained down bombs on London. The long months of waiting were over. This was what had been expected just a year ago. London was now the front line.